PART ONE

SPIRITUALLY TRANSFORMATIVE EXPERIENCES

NAVIGATING THE WONDROUS HOLY SH*T SHOW OF AWAKENING

A GUIDE FOR INDIVIDUALS, SPIRITUAL LEADERS, PRACTITIONERS, AND MEDIA

MARY REED

This book is available on Amazon.com.
ISBN: 9798328044240

Cover and interior layout and sketch art by Cheri Warren.
Cover and interior circle art by Rashani Réa.
Cover poop emoji by Ashlee Eikelboom.

This book is specifically intended to provide loving support for:

▷ Individuals processing the impact of transformative metaphysical events such as near-death experiences, spontaneous awakenings, otherworldly mystical insights or journeys, Kundalini activations, and so on.

▷ Individuals who have not had profound transformative events but are in transitional stages of awakening such as feeling stuck, directionless, or spiritually called to something deeper in their relationships, work, community, or self.

▷ Practitioners and leaders in the field of mental health, wellness, and spirituality providing support for the above individuals.

▷ Media representatives who interview individuals having awakening experiences or who explore the subject of awakening in public forums.

ABOUT THE TITLE

One morning I went for a walk while wearing a blue t-shirt adorned with an image of a plump unicorn. Above the unicorn were the words MAGICAL AF. Shortly, a petite elderly woman with meticulously sculpted snow-white hair stopped me as she passed by. She said, "May I ask, what does 'AF' stand for?"

I said, "Well, back in the day you and I probably would have said 'as all get out.' But I think young people figured out it was more fun to be naughty and say 'as fuck.'"

The woman's eyes shot open wide. "Oh!" she exclaimed. Then, in a split second, I watched delight dawn on her like permission arriving from somewhere in her brain to find this funny. She smirked as she turned to walk away and said, "Well, how about that."

The title for this book includes the term "shit show" because it is more fun and light-spirited than words like "messy" and "chaotic." But it is also more *cathartically honest* when speaking about the full scope of spiritual awakening. Our awakening journeys are indeed wondrous and holy, but we have for too long dressed up spirituality in nice-only terms, when in truth it is often deeply confusing and painful. When we use terms that *energetically* convey the truth of our lived experience more deeply, it is easier for us to feel truly seen in our confusion and pain.

Spiritual awakening can help us see how we have separated ourselves from Divine truth by piously believing that a nicely packaged world is the only one that is holy. We place not-nice words and painful truths outside of Divine Love, and then we live comfortably righteous in that separation mindset. Awakening is inciting in us the *visceral remembrance* that everything is of Source/God. Every word, every truth, every experience is holy. Every tiny bit of our wondrous shit show of spiritual awakening is holy. And I aim to honor that truth with joyful abandon in this text.

ABOUT THE AUTHOR

More than two decades ago, I was a staunchly agnostic healthcare executive in Washington, DC. That normal life began to veer off track in December 2000 when I started having uncontrollable mystical experiences with the likes of Jesus, Buddha and angels. I spent ten years in profound confusion, unable to find anyone who could help me understand what was happening. That chaos became unbearable just as every aspect of my normal life fell apart, and the weight of my despair led to a suicide attempt in March 2011. Inexplicably, two days after taking ninety-six pain and sleeping pills with three glasses of wine alone in my home, I woke up. I had no options left then but to surrender in defeat and stop trying to reject or control or understand what was happening.

In that authentic state of allowance, I was invited to India to tell my story to a high Tibetan lama, and did not return home for seven years. I spent most of that time living in a remote Buddhist nunnery in the Himalayas coming to terms with my true calling. This journey of self-acceptance is detailed in my memoir, *Unwitting Mystic: Evolution of the Message of Love.*

Today I am a mystic wisdom guide, and author of four books on spiritual awakening. I work with people around the world who are at varying stages of their spiritual evolution, and I host weekly online teachings for members of my private community. I know firsthand the range of challenges we face in our individual and collective transformation, and I also know the incredible relief, joy and freedom that come with Divinely-inspired support.

More information about my work is available at lovemaryreed.com.

CONTENTS

The AWAKENING TRAIN
has left the station and it
HAS NO BRAKES

It is not hard to see there is a momentum of awakening to higher levels of consciousness going on in our world. There is widespread rebellion against old oppressive systems that govern human life, and widespread social and technological changes catalyzed by vastly more creative and collaborative thinking than in the past. There is also widespread resistance to all of this. Humanity isn't exactly winning the cosmic Most Gracefully Evolving Species prize, but we are, even if clumsily, making our way out of eons of painful beliefs and paradigms that have dictated our ways of life.

Today countless individuals around the world are experiencing ever-expanding levels of awareness, understanding, healing, and potential. Whether we suddenly find ourselves in otherworldly events or gradually find ourselves facing deep personal realizations, these are points of no return to an old sense of self and life. We can't un-experience an experience or un-know a truth. We can try to ignore or suppress these things, but in our hearts we know we are changed.

These shifts are opportunities for transcendence and healing, but first they will bring to our awareness the limitations to be transcended and the pain to be healed. Sorting through these issues and integrating new perspectives can be a challenging and confusing process as we seek to understand who and what we are now. This book provides helpful information for people in the throes of these challenges, as well as guidance for those aiming to support these individuals or promote understanding of our awakening world.

I make a distinction in this text between two general paths of spiritual awakening: one that propels people along rather dramatically through transformative metaphysical experiences, and one that unfolds more gradually (and therefore often more arduously) without these experiences. These are two very different paths, each with their own promise and plight, and it is important to understand what is happening in both.

The information I provide comes from two decades of direct personal experience with profound metaphysical events and my work with more than a thousand people in varying stages of awakening. What I share may or may not be corroborated by research, other teachers, or others who are in the throes of spiritual awakening; I am only able to speak from my own firsthand experience and the experiences of those with whom I have worked. (Dozens of my own experiences and select stories from my work are detailed in my other books.)

In this text I do not attempt to correlate types of experiences with specific stages of awakening, levels of consciousness, or dimensions of existence that have been demarcated by others. The mind tends to use that kind of information as a challenge to pursue what is perceived to be a more prestigious state, rejecting all the incredible wisdom and healing available in one's present state. We have enough things in our world telling us we need to do more or be better; I do not need to add to that noise. It is okay for us to be wherever we are in our spiritual journey, even if we are all over the place. My aim is to honor and support people wherever they are, and to help them realize through their own lived experience that, in truth, Divine potential is limitless, and wherever they are is both sacred space and a sacred doorway to exploring ever more of that truth.

Lastly, my personal and work experiences do not capture every possible scenario or concern that can happen in spiritual awakening; everyone is different and every path traverses a unique landscape. But my hope is that what I share compels compassionate understanding and support for anyone on the leading edge of humanity's great shift in consciousness, and that the information fosters a deeper appreciation for all the holy wonder and shit that our precious world is going through on the way to healing and wholeness.

COMMON ELEMENTS OF

Chapter 1

SPIRITUALLY TRANSFORMATIVE EXPERIENCES

For a growing number of people, awakening is happening through catapulting events commonly referred to as spiritually transformative experiences (STEs). These are *embodied* metaphysical events that can incite profound realizations about ourselves, the world we live in, and dimensions beyond narrow definitions of "reality." They can also illuminate perspectives that refute the vast array of limiting beliefs that have historically shaped the human experience. These potent events can happen unexpectedly in near-death experiences, spontaneous metaphysical experiences, and hypnagogic (pre-sleep) or hypnopompic (post-sleep) states, and they can happen more deliberately through endeavors such as psychedelic journeys (e.g. ayahuasca, LSD), spiritual rituals and practices, hypnosis, and deeply meditative states.

To be clear, I speak here about authentic transformative events in which one is fully immersed energetically in the experience, not events that one mentally imagines or deludes. The energetic difference between these embodied-versus-mental events is, on the mild end of the continuum, as distinguishable as the experience of describing what it is like to eat a lime versus actually eating a lime. On the intense end of the continuum, the energetic difference is as distinguishable as the difference between describing what it is like to birth a baby versus actually birthing a baby. We have distinctly *visceral* awareness in an STE, and the information revealed or conveyed is usually profound, simple, surprising, and something our mind does not fathom. Further, authentic STEs do not incite or encourage conflict, judgment, oppression, inequality or violence, since the *source* of the event is Divine Love.

"The range of phenomena that can happen in spiritually transformative experiences is infinite, and no two events are alike."

(Though, in rare instances when one has to transcend extensive energetic imprints of fear for their vibration to rise, the STE can start out fearful.)

With the growing availability of offerings that can incite transformative experiences, and the rapidly expanding collective consciousness that can naturally foster them, these events are becoming more common and are being discussed publicly more than ever before. Therefore it is important to understand what STEs are and how their impact can dramatically change one's life.

The range of phenomena that can happen in spiritually transformative experiences is infinite, and no two events are alike. There are, however, common elements often involved, including:

- **A light**. A light often appears that is very bright or of a unique color. The size of the light can range from tiny and pin-like to massive and all encompassing. The light may have palpable qualities such as warmth, emotion, love, and/or a sense of personification. Some experiencers feel a pull towards, or invitation into, the light.

- **A tunnel.** Many people have a sense of traveling in a forward motion through a tunnel to a different space or realm. (Though I personally went through a tunnel backwards.) While the tunnel is usually bright light, some experience it as a tunnel of darkness.

- **A voice or telepathic communication.** A voice or communication often comes from no apparent source, but can also emanate from one or more entities conveying information with or without words being spoken.

> *"We realize that separation is either an illusion or a choice to experience an individual 'I' that believes it is separate from its source."*

- **Absence of a self or form or identity.** It is common to have a sense of being without a physical body. Some experience becoming light, or as a point of awareness within a greater field or as the field itself, or as something altogether different. Some may see their physical body but have a sense of being separate from it. Often an experiencer realizes through this not-in-body awareness that they are not their human identity and they have simply been playing a character on Earth.

- **Otherworldly sounds, colors, symbols, lights or movements.** These features often appear exquisitely "more" than an earthly experience, as in sounds that are angelic and colors that have never been seen before. These features also commonly convey information, or evoke deep understandings, emotions or memories.

Presence of Source/God/Creator. Many encounter what they perceive to be God or Creator, or a sense of All That Is. Some also experience themselves as, inseparable from, or an expression of, this Source presence. This presence usually radiates exquisite unconditional love that is commonly imbued with astounding joy, playfulness, and/or equanimous peace. (I have personally never experienced God as judgmental, vengeful, condemning or angry, nor have I ever worked with anyone who has.)

- **Union or telepathic communication with nature, animals, objects, or other people**. This usually happens in a waking state when we look at, or think about, something or someone and suddenly unite or connect deeply with the consciousness or essence of that object or being. There is often information conveyed in the connection, and an understanding that we are inherently one with the consciousness of everything. (I have personally come into full union with a person who was nowhere near me, with nature where I was hiking, and with objects in a bedroom. In each experience, entirely new levels of profound information were conveyed and I had completely different levels of abilities to perceive.)

- **Sudden realization that separation is an illusion or choice**. When we have an experience of unity consciousness — being one with/as All That Is or nature, animals, objects, other people, or other entities — we realize that separation is either an illusion or an intentional choice to experience an individual "I" that believes it is separate from its source.

- **Appearance of a relative, loved one, or stranger**. These appearances include relatives known and unknown, living or dead, as well as strangers or loved ones who are living or dead. Usually these beings come as guides or have a specific message.

- **Presence of discarnate beings**. Many people encounter beings of light or other personified forms and shapes. Some people also experience themselves as, or part of, or cosmically connected to, these entities. As with the Source/God/Creator presence, these beings, too, often radiate powerful love, joy, wisdom, playfulness and/or peace.

- **Travel to, or sudden presence in, other places or other lives**. Some can experience a sense of journeying to or through alternative scenes/realms/dimensions/lives, while others find themselves suddenly in new environments without a feeling of having traveled there. (Near-death experiencer and author Natalie Sudman brilliantly refers to the latter as "blink environments.")

- **Sense of timelessness**. An absence of the concept of time is very common in STEs. To the mind it may feel like the experience goes on for minutes, days, or even years, when in earthly time only seconds or minutes or even no time at all has passed.

> *"There is sometimes a sense of 'cracking open' or a loosening of energy that has been stuck."*

- **A sense of great vastness or expansion**. Many experience a sense of vast space or expansive being. This is often seen or felt within a cosmos or galaxies or endless stars, though some also experience more ground-based environments such as meadows, forests, and oceans.

- **Physical sensations in the body**. This can be anything from minor tingling to uncontrolled muscle movements, but it is most common to feel energy flowing in a distinct direction or pattern. Potent energy may fill or swell in the body, or radiate through specific places in the body (upward movement in the spine is often called a Kundalini awakening). There is sometimes a sense of "cracking open" or a loosening of energy that has been stuck, and in these experiences people may notice spontaneous healings of various illnesses or conditions. There also may be a sense that something is being rearranged in the body or mind, like a tweaking or updating or releasing of some old internal pattern.

Piercing humor and playfulness. Contrary to what most people might expect, "masters," otherworldly beings and Source/God are often experienced as extremely lighthearted and fun. The purity of love contained in their playfulness creates an immediate sense of profound ease and relief. (I have cried deeply at simply a wink from God, a smile from Buddha, a joke from Archangel Michael, and teasing laughter from my soul group.)

- **Remembrance of repressed memories**. These memories may be from this lifetime or what may be perceived to be pre-birth, past, or parallel life memories. There is almost always something significant about one's current life that is realized through these memories, but there can also be simply a "popcorn" effect of random memories popping up when energetic imprints within one's vibrational field release.

- **Hyper reality**. The otherworldly realms often feel far more real than our earthly reality. The juxtaposition between these realities can add to the difficulty in coming back from an STE because it is like stepping out of a richly depicted oil painting and into a pencil sketch. (When my metaphysical experiences first began, every time I came back from an STE I felt like I was being stuffed into a glass Coke bottle; this reality felt oppressively tight and distorted.)

- **A life review**. This is an eye- and heart-opening experience of seeing our life from a higher perspective, and understanding the impact of our actions and choices. Often we get to see or re-live not only our own actions and choices but the impact of those actions and choices on others. Importantly, we usually realize in this experience that the only judgment present in the review is coming from ourselves, not from God or any Divine entity that may be present.

- **Sudden expansive knowing or understanding**. This often feels like a surprising aha! that allows one to realize they've been blind to simple truths about themselves, others, the world, or greater spiritual wisdom. It can also be experienced as a large download of information (often instantaneously), which the experiencer may or may not be able to bring back to their earthly life and remember in full. In the latter instance people may recover the information in bits and pieces over time.

- **A feeling of dying or a sense that one's life is finished.** In an event that does not involve actual physical death, this sense of dying or finality is often felt as an "ego death" when there is a deep internal shift towards a greater awareness of a Higher Self. In near-death experiences, however, there can be the awareness of physical death followed by an understanding (usually in an alternative dimension) that one's physical life is not actually finished. In these cases one may be given the choice to return to their body or be told they must return because it is not their time yet.

> *"Scary realms or entities are often a kind of gateway path that lead to healing realms."*

Whether or not one is allowed the choice to return apparently depends on several factors, including one's life purpose or priorities, one's "soul contracts" with other beings, and one's pre-birth plans.

- **Terrifying scenes or beings.** In rare cases, one can experience what appear to be hellish realms or scary entities. These rare events are often associated with deep imprints of fear in one's energetic field, either through religious or cultural indoctrination of terrifying ideas such as hell, damnation, and evil, or through self-association with these ideas because of one's own history (e.g. soldiers or others who have been party to terror for others or themselves). In these rare experiences, the scary realms or entities are often a kind of gateway path that lead to healing realms. Some report this feels like a process of moving through a dense, dark layer of energy in order to reach a more spacious and luminous field. Some experiencers also report feeling that a terrifying event was understood as a transcendent experience being witnessed through the *filter or angle of perception* of fear. In these cases there is usually a realization that the filter can be removed, or the angle of perception shifted, and the experience becomes wondrous and inviting.

A WORD OF CAUTION ABOUT DISCERNING A SPIRITUAL EXPERIENCE FROM A MENTAL DISTURBANCE: Authentic spiritually transformative experiences are almost always a profoundly loving, transcendent event. While in rare cases an STE may have fearful components or initial stages, experiences that are heavily based in terror, paranoia, or aggression are more likely an event caused by mental instability. Signs that this may be the case include:

• There was no sense of profound love or transcendent calming awareness experienced in the event.
• Intense fear, paranoia or aggression continue after the event.
• The experiencer has a history of mental instability.

If any of these conditions are met, it is best to seek support from a mental health professional as soon as possible after the event. That said, it is important to note that just because someone has a history of mental instability or has a fearful experience does not mean their experience was not an authentic STE. It will be important to connect with a mental health professional who can discern the difference. (See resources in Chapter Three.)

COMMON CHALLENGES THAT FOLLOW

Chapter 2

SPIRITUALLY TRANSFORMATIVE EXPERIENCES

Immediately after an STE, experiencers often have an acute period of gratitude, joy, awe, and even ecstasy. During this time we can feel dazed and distracted to varying degrees as highly activated energies within us are still settling. Very often we have a lingering coursing-through-the-body sense of profound love and a knowing that our purpose is to love. While heightened energies still linger, some people notice they can see auras around objects and people, or know things psychically, or have other types of expanded perception.

While in some cases this "fully in it" state remains constant, for most people the acute period of connection usually lasts anywhere from a few days to a few months before questioning, doubt and confusion start to creep in. This is when many of us find ourselves in front row seats at the shit show. Some of the challenges include:

꙰ **Coming back.** In STEs where we experience immense love, joy, peace, understanding, and/or exquisite Divine realms, it can be devastating to have to come back and live in our earthly reality again. After our initial period of excitement and wonder, it is not uncommon to experience grief, depression, and/or anger at how hard earthly life feels, comparatively speaking. In STEs where we meet God, it can be especially devastating to separate from such a profound presence because the unconditional love and profound sense of belonging and acceptance we feel is beyond any version of love, belonging and acceptance we experience on earth, and the juxtaposition can be excruciating.

⚛ **Can't remember or make sense of everything that happened**. Countless things can happen in a single STE, and often we can only remember or make sense of bits and pieces. With time more clarity can come, but until then it can be deeply confusing to try to make sense of things when important information seems to be missing.

⚛ **Continued episodes of expanded awareness**. While energies are still high within us we can continue to have a wide range of metaphysical experiences in our waking states. This can be both destabilizing and disorienting because we haven't gotten grounded yet from our initial experience and we have a sense of not being fully "here" yet.

⚛ **Chasing the high**. In STEs where there is a profound sense of peace, ecstasy, love, or healing, many experiencers will try again and again to get back to that high. This is usually done either through induced journeys (e.g. drugs) or relentless spiritual practices. However, very rarely is the person able to sate their yearning. This chase-the-high process not only feels unsatisfying and frustrating, it also keeps the person emotionally and mentally unbalanced because there is a chronic incitement of energies, so one's energetic field has no chance for things to settle and integrate.

⚛ **Can't aptly describe the experience in words**. It is extremely hard to thoroughly convey everything that happens in an STE. The scale and depth of what happens is far greater than can be distilled into words, and the *pure* qualities of the experience defy human definition or understanding. It is like trying to describe an orange using language only meant for avocados: the general subject may be understood to be about food, but the words and concepts are neither right nor enough. This is especially frustrating because talking about what happened is often a deep need for experiencers; it is the way we seek to process the shock, wonder, and/or confusion.

🔸 **Fear of speaking up about what happened**. While most may feel a deep need to talk about their experiences as a way to process the event, many are afraid to disclose their truth for fear of judgment or rejection. This is especially challenging for people raised in religious or cultural environments where something like an STE is considered crazy, blasphemous, or a sign of evil.

🔸 **Confusion is compounded by those we turn to for help**. While this issue is gradually getting better, there is still a vast poverty of trained therapists, doctors, guides, and ministers who have the understanding and skills necessary to adeptly support experiencers through the impact and integration of

"As old energetic patterns release and new ones infuse, our entire energetic field is finding new balance."

their STE. (Thus the need for resources like this book.) Practitioners and ministers often have personal or professional bias or judgment when it comes to metaphysical matters, and the same challenge with bias, judgment, and lack of resources for greater understanding is also common for our friends and family as well. The lack of safety or understanding one can experience when sharing their stories can be both oppressive and traumatic.

🙏 **Feeling emotional/mentally unbalanced.** In addition to the instability incited by chasing the high, an STE often disrupts and even dissolves old mental patterns — our thoughts, impulses, reactions, beliefs and perspectives — which can cause us to feel disoriented, ungrounded, and emotionally all over the place. Some people also begin processing emotions they have tried to repress for much of their life but now can't hold back, especially grief, sadness and anger.

🙏 **Dreams become intensely strange or wondrous.** Because these experiences are energetically potent, often the processing of that energetic influence continues during sleep in the days and weeks following an STE. As old energetic patterns release and new ones infuse, our entire energetic field is finding new balance, and sleep allows all of this to happen most easily. During this time our dreams can become rich in strange or wondrous imagery or emotional impact.

🙏 **Concern that we are crazy or that we made the experience up.** Since these experiences are unusual and not yet thought of as normal or commonplace by most people and institutions, we can tend to believe the event was a product of imagination or mental instability. This is often compounded by messages we receive from others who tell us that this is the case.

🙏 **Confused about what to do with the information gleaned.** In events where incredible healing information is realized, there is often a deep desire or sense of obligation to *DO* something with that information so that others can benefit from it. This can create a heavy or urgent sense of responsibility, which can be overwhelming if we are trying to bring something big or impactful to the world before we have fully integrated our experience and truly understand what the *application* of it actually might be.

⚵ **Ego taking control of the narrative and application of the STE**. Our ego will seek to fill in gaps in our understanding or abilities with what it deduces or assumes must be right. It will seek to explain the STE from the perspective of what the mind figured out *about it*, rather than through the actual experience itself. Our ego's eager desire to *do* something with the information we glean in an STE can lead us to offer healing or awakening "services" before we are ready. When the well-meaning ego has information it thinks is right, helpful, or marketable, it can get to work using the experience before we have fully integrated all that happened, thus adding to our own confusion and to the confusion of those we serve.

"While we are sorting through thoughts and feelings that can be overwhelming, the world around us can also feel overwhelming."

⚵ **Sense of being special or chosen**. Some people are told or shown they have a specific mission on earth (e.g share XYZ message). Others are given specific new skills or abilities (e.g. new language or higher perceptions). The challenge is that, to the mind, being given these specific missions or skills is an indication that we are special or chosen, when in fact, we are simply being aligned with our particular individual path or calling.

⚜ **Desire to isolate**. While we are sorting through thoughts and feelings that can be overwhelming, the world around us can also feel overwhelming. It is not uncommon after an STE to feel better alone in our own environment than with others in public settings. This can make going to work or engaging socially quite challenging. It can also make it difficult to face everyday responsibilities that require us to engage with others, such as picking the kids up from school or going to the store.

⚜ **Feeling exhausted or sick from having to be "normal."** Related to the above, when we are still integrating the expansive energies of an STE it can be extremely difficult to focus our attention through what feels like the tiny vessel of a body or the limited "I" mind. That level of effort can cause fatigue, nausea and a need for prolonged periods of rest to allow one's internal world to acclimate.

⚜ **Frustrations of feeling stuck, directionless, or depressed**. Many people go through a heavy stage of questioning the purpose of their STE when they don't seem to have any clear direction in life afterwards. This, coupled often with an inability to "reconnect" metaphysically, can lead to feeling stuck, directionless, or depressed.

⚜ **Life priorities may change**. It is common for experiencers to see their life in a new light after an STE. What once was tolerated may become intolerable. Goals may change or disappear entirely. We may begin to align our choices with what feels like higher purpose or potential. We can find it difficult to work or engage through the intellect instead of the heart. All of these things can impact our relationships, jobs, family, and community life, and they can create a sense of feeling lost because we do not know our "new" self yet, we only know the old self is no longer in charge.

"Often it is not just one thing unpredictably changing it is many things."

🔹 **Life as we knew it falls apart**. Related to the above, while we know things have shifted within us, sometimes that internal shift prompts changes we are either not ready for or even considering. This can be an extremely challenging time, as things in our life can abruptly shift directions and we have no idea what is happening. Often it is not just one thing unpredictably changing, it is many things, and we cannot seem to do anything to find our way back to normalcy. This phase can feel deeply confusing and we can feel quite lost. (This phase was described to me by psychologist Dr. Rudy Bauer like this: When the light of the Divine hits the darkness of the mind, as in an STE, the light fractures that darkness. And sometimes that fracturing then manifests in the circumstances of our life.)

🔹 **Post Traumatic Stress Disorder or PTSD-like symptoms**. In some STEs, the shock is so sudden and/or the impact is so immense that it is a traumatic experience. This is especially the case when one has faced physical death or the rare hellish experience, but it can also happen with exquisitely blissful events. This trauma can be compounded when, as mentioned earlier, one shares their experience with others who do not understand or believe the event.

TIPS TO HELP INTEGRATE

SPIRITUALLY TRANSFORMATIVE
EXPERIENCES

Whatever the nature of any STE may be, it is first and foremost transformative. These events deeply affect our old way of understanding ourselves and our world, and the impact can jolt our mind and heart so powerfully it is not possible to go back to our old way of being.

This transformative impact is why it is important to understand that:

> *integration is the most vital part of every experience and every awakening journey.*

Every event, every new understanding, takes time to absorb and become integral to who and how we are. It takes time to allow the experience to ease out of our mind, where we obsessively replay and analyze and seek to understand what happened, and into the very fabric of our being. It takes time for all that we experienced to naturally reshape our understanding of our True Self.

A single transformative experience can take many years to integrate. Several psychotherapists I sought help from in my early years said research showed the average time for integration was around seven years, and in my experience that was about right for most of my large scale STEs. Today, however, it seems that timeframe may be getting shorter since far more information is available to help with the process and we have evolved enough collectively now to allow greater perspectives and possibilities into our awareness more readily. But regardless of how much time it takes, the integration process is extremely important and cannot be rushed. Therefore it is imperative to know what to expect and how to help manage the integration process.

◎ **Remember your integration process will unfold gradually**. In the same way we grew up acclimating to life incrementally from childhood to adulthood, in the aftermath of an STE we are acclimating incrementally from adulthood to Divinehood. There is a great deal of energy being rearranged and reoriented within us, so we need to give ourselves plenty of space and time to feel confused, curious, and all the other things dotting the continuum from sad to ecstatic. We cannot rush ourselves any more than we can rush the unfolding of seasons, so it helps to welcome time as a compassionate teacher guiding us into ever deeper capacities to relax, trust, and embrace the journey. STEs are exceptional teachers of trust and patience.

◎ **Whether, when and how to talk about your experience with others will be one of the most important factors in your integration journey**. Take time to allow your internal guidance to help you discern when and how to start opening up to others, keeping in mind:

- Others may, in fact, doubt or judge you, but their opinions do not invalidate your truth.

- Fear of judgment can cloud what you say or cause self-doubt. Note when you are feeling limited, and let that awareness guide you to know when the time is right to speak freely.

- Others may not only believe you but think your experience gives you the ability to answer their life questions or solve their problems. Remember what you *truly* know, be honest about what you *do not* truly know, and be aware when your ego is trying to fill in the gaps. You will know when you are speaking from experience versus assumption, so take the time to let truth be your guide. This is especially helpful if you do public interviews, as many people will hear your words and you will want to feel comfortable in your accountability.

Allow the truth of your experience to speak its own purity. You do not need to shape or minimize the details of your experience to fit anyone else's comfort levels. The truth came to you in the way it did because it is seeking to be known, not masked or hidden or reshaped to be more acceptable to others.

- Speak only in the way and format that feels most comfortable for you. You may start by sharing your experience with a friend over coffee, but writing and/or speaking more widely may also be cathartic and helpful. It takes time to find the right words or phrasing, and narrating things can often help incite even deeper remembrance of details. Feel into what aligns with your comfort level for sharing, and when the time is right you'll know whether to open the door to sharing more publicly through social media posts, blogs, essays, a book, public talks, podcasts or the like. Note that it can be extremely helpful to start small and work your way into the public arena.

- Be aware that your ego may be eager to use your experience to fix or save others or convince them they are wrong. You can hold your truth and meet people where they are in their truth without either of you needing to be any different.

- Remember that you and your experience have worth, and your story may help others like yourself who seek to be seen and understood. When you're ready to share, others will be ready for you.

◎ **Find someone to talk to who can support you not just in processing the shock of your STE, but in your journey of integration and evolution.** This may be a therapist, a guide, a teacher, a mentor, a practitioner, a minister, or a combination of these. (I ended up with two therapists who had different skillsets and coordinated my care.) Finding the right person or people can take time and be a frustrating lesson in what *doesn't* feel helpful, but it is incredibly comforting and stabilizing when we do find the right support. This is especially important for those experiencing PTSD symptoms or depression.

◎ **Community can also be incredibly important in grounding, comforting, and stabilizing**. There are communities around the world now where spiritually transformative experiences resonate; where our range of emotions and confusion are supported and no one is trying to fit us into a box. Good places to explore community options include:

✓ Spiritual centers that have a sincere all-are-welcome policy. Non-denominational centers tend to be more inclusive and open to embracing the perspectives we glean in STEs. (If you were already part of a religious or spiritual community prior to your experience you may find yourself seeing that community differently now.)

✓ Online interview programs and podcasts that focus on spiritual awakening and STEs. Often the hosts or guests have their own communities you can join, or they offer information about other communities that may be of interest.

✓ Books on spiritual awakening or STEs, as often the author hosts their own community gatherings (as I do).

✓ Spiritual retreats can also be great environments to learn about different communities from either the venue, the hosts, or attendees.

A WORD OF CAUTION ABOUT SPIRITUAL TEACHERS, LEADERS AND COMMUNITIES: Today there are many people offering spiritual guidance and support, and some are very skilled and insightful in their service. However, spiritual teachers, guides or leaders and their communities are prone to the same struggles with awakening that you are. While their intentions may be to serve, often times what is doing the serving is more ego than spirit. This can create complications for anyone who puts their trust in these individuals, especially when one is already in a vulnerable and confused state following an STE. Authentic guides and teachers do not lead through fear, exploitation, manipulation, or guess work. They do not put themselves on a pedestal to be revered, and they do not mandate that you turn your decision making or life path over to them. Authentic teachers empower their students, fostering remembrance of, and resonance with, the Divine wisdom we all innately hold within — and they will guide their communities in this same empowering way. So, trust what resonates and pay attention to any warning signs that may indicate disempowerment, exploitation, manipulation, or ineptitude. Let YOUR truth, YOUR power be your guide.

◎ **Explore courses or workshops that feel interesting or exciting.** These can be a great way to explore more of the perspectives, potential, or capabilities you realized in your experience. They can also be a great way to meet other experiencers or people who resonate with your story. However, be mindful of not using these endeavors to chase the high of your STE, as noted in chapter two. That will only keep things stirred up while your body and mind are still trying to integrate the impact of your experience.

◎ **Treatments or programs that help care for your body and energy can be helpful in fostering physical balance and wellbeing**. Your body is processing a great deal of internal change from the energetic influence of your STE. Treatments such as massage, craniosacral therapy, sound baths, yoga or other movement modalities, as well as energy balancing techniques like acupuncture and biofield tuning can be highly effective in calming, centering, and grounding the body and mind.

◎ **In addition to care for the body, it is extremely helpful to explore techniques that can help calm and center the mind**. Meditation can be very effective, but different people resonate with different practices. Explore the array of meditation options available such as guided, mantra or chanting, silence, transcendental, breath work, and other techniques to see what feels good for you.

"You are in a going-through process, not a stuck-in process."

(Note that it is likely NOT helpful to do a deep dive into intense multi-day meditation programs such as Vipassana before you have stabilized from your STE.) It is also helpful to ground yourself in earthly activities such as being in nature and gardening, and in creative activities such as painting, music, cooking, crafts, and so on. This moves energy through the body without the mind directing the show.

◎ **Avoid use of substances or rituals to chase the high or bypass the confusion**. This only makes integration harder and the confusion go on longer. Trying to rush the awakening journey or shortcut the integration process leads to chronic instability because energies are constantly being incited and the entire energetic field has no way to settle into a balanced state.

◎ **Consider allopathic medications for support if your body and mind become exhausted.** Many people eschew antidepressants and other allopathic treatments, but in some cases they can be a helpful temporary resource to get us through extreme periods of depression or instability.

◎ **Take time to let things settle to the point where you feel balanced and steady before "doing" something with the information or capacities gleaned in your experience.** It will take time to come into your capacity to be of service from a state of awareness that is fully aligned with your Divine truth and purpose. If you leap into offering services before you are ready there's a good chance your ego will complicate things for you and those you aim to help. It will rely more heavily on intellect than intuitive connection, and not allow you to easily yield to higher potential or trust. You will recognize when you are ready to begin offering services when it feels like that is the next natural step, and opportunities to serve will start showing up readily.

"As you stand in your truth you become a beacon of remembrance and potential for others."

◎ **Keep in mind that you are in a going-through process of integration, not a stuck-in process.** Remember to lean into the love, wonder and joy of your experience and let that feeling be your companion throughout your journey.

◎ **Remember that you do not need friends or family or anyone else to validate your STE or be where you are in your spiritual awakening**. You can invite others to watch videos or read books to better understand your experience, but they have their own journey and are evolving in their own way just as you are. As you stand in your truth you become a beacon of remembrance and potential for others.

Have fun recalling your extraordinary experience. While the confusion and integration of an STE can at times be intense, remember that in this human lifetime you experienced something absolutely *AMAZING*. Let yourself bask in the wonder and *fun* of such an incredibly transformative gift!

In addition to the tips already listed, there are countless resources that can offer more personalized support or specific information for you. To mention just a few:

- The International Association of Near-Death Studies (IANDS.org). This organization offers a wide variety of information pertaining to STEs (primarily NDEs but they are evolving), and they hold an annual conference in which experiencers and people working in, or interested in, the field of consciousness and spiritual awakening can meet and inspire each other.

- Spiritual Emergence Network https://www.spiritualemergence.org/. This is a network of over 200 therapists and other professionals specializing in helping people with difficult spiritual experiences. This provides a directory for people seeking psycho-spiritual support following a spiritual crisis or big experience.

- Buddha at the Gas Pump (BATGAP.com). This online program interviews a wide variety of people in their awakening journeys and professionals who work in the field of consciousness. The focus can at times be too intellectual for those who prefer less analysis and more personal experience, but importantly, the BATGAP website has a categorical index of interviewees that includes psychotherapists and teachers who are well versed in spiritual awakening.

- Online programs such as Next Level Soul (nextlevelsoul.com). Programs like these showcase STE experiencers from around the world and thoughtfully explore the subject of spiritual awakening from a wide variety of angles. The stories and discussions can help you see your STE and your journey in a different light. I highlight the Next Level Soul program here because the host does not frame stories in a religious or doctrine-based light. There are many other programs like this whose hosts succeed to varying degrees in questioning their guests thoughtfully without an agenda of their own. (Religious or doctrine-based online programs abound, but I have no experience with them.)

- The Washington Center for Consciousness Studies (meditatelive.com). For those compelled to explore meditation and consciousness through the lens of eastern traditions and teachers, Dr. Rudy Bauer offers many free meditation videos and opportunities to meditate virtually with others on a daily basis. Dr. Bauer is an expert in psychotherapeutic work involving spiritual phenomenology, and is an excellent resource to help discern between an authentic STE and a mental disturbance event.

- Books that show the scale of possibilities and potential offered through STEs. There are many inspiring stories available in book form now; a few examples include: *The Application of Impossible Things* by Natalie Sudman, *A Walk in the Physical* by Christian Sundberg, *Proof of Heaven* by Eben Alexander, and my own books *Unwitting Mystic* and *Humanity's Epic Awakening.* Seeing your own journey and understandings reflected in these stories can reconnect you to the wonder and awe you experienced in your STE.

- Specifically for STEs that are prompted by psychedelics, the book *Psychedelic Integration: Psychotherapy for Non-ordinary States of Consciousness* by Marc Aixal is a helpful resource for both experiencers and psychotherapists.

- Suicide hotlines and crisis support. If your despair gets to be too much there is help available. Wikipedia provides worldwide contact information for suicide hotlines at

- en.wikipedia.org/wiki/List_of_suicide_crisis_lines. Renowned sound healer Tom Kenyon has a suicide prevention program that works to ease the brain patterns contributing to despairing thoughts (tomkenyon.com/suicide-prevention). For those dealing with particularly relentless PTSD or depression, medications may be a helpful bridge to get you through peak intense periods of integration, and these should be discussed with your mental health provider.

WHAT TO LOOK FORWARD TO

AS THINGS INTEGRATE

As the confusion and chaotic thoughts begin to settle down, we start to become aware that we have changed or are being evermore drawn to change in numerous ways. We begin to realize that some things about us or our life have simply dropped away and other things have become part of our new normal. We still have ups and downs, but we have an ever-greater capacity to manage the challenges without getting knocked off balance. Common changes we notice as we evolve through deeper integration of our STE include:

- **Trust that we are of a loving God/Source/ Consciousness**. For those who experienced evidence of love, compassion and wisdom that far exceed earthly ideas of these things, as our confusion lessens it becomes easier to trust that we are inherently part of a unitive Consciousness. We trust that we are expressions of an unconditionally loving Source/God. This can be a significant shift for those who were previously agnostic or atheist, and a healing experience for those who grew up in religions that teach of a vengeful, judging, or conquering god.

- **Feeling peaceful, calm and content**. In time, our state of being becomes less agitated and more even-keeled. We begin to notice that we wake up feeling lighter and have a growing sense of internal ease throughout the day.

- **Deeper ability to accept self, others, and situations**. Our old impulses of judgment usually become less intense or frequent. We have a greater capacity to accept people and circumstances as they are rather than needing them to be different to make us feel better. This process begins with heightened awareness that our old reactionary habits have waned, and we grow evermore aware that we are evolving into a more gentle way of relating to self and others.

- **Increased ability to love oneself unconditionally**. For some experiencers, the ability to love oneself is immediate because our STE immersed us in true knowing of our Divine nature and innate worthiness. For most people, however, this ability unfolds over time as the integration of the STE incites deeper remembrance of our Divine nature and worthiness.

> *"It is very common for experiencers to lose interest in any form of conflict that once would have vied for their attention."*

- **Ability to find more beauty and wonder in the world**. Most experiencers get evidence that there is beauty and wonder beyond what we can see with our earthly vision. As our thoughts become less cluttered and judgmental, the evidence we received in the STE can foster an ability to see more deeply into what is right before our eyes. We recognize and appreciate the weave of interdependence in our world, and how incredible it is to be part of, and blessed by, the interplay of all things.

- **Increased capacity to feel connected to Higher Self, Divine guides, and deeper wisdom**. As we become less focused through the mind that generates and perpetuates confusion, we find ourselves dropping deeper into intuitive awareness. This is enhanced for those who feel drawn to meditative practices that quiet the mind and allow a more discerning state of internal awareness.

Remembrance of our playful nature. The realms and beings present in an STE commonly have a potent sense of lightness, ease and even humor. Experiencing the impact of these things in such a pure setting can reconnect us to this aspect to our Divine nature; we remember that we are, inherently, joyful beings. With this aspect of our nature brought to our awareness, as confusion decreases we often find ourselves feeling more lighthearted or drawn to more lighthearted influences and people. We develop an ever-deepening appreciation for the whimsy that is playfully sprinkled throughout life.

- **Less interested in conflict in any form**. It is very common for experiencers to lose interest in any form of conflict that once would have vied for their attention. This includes mass media news, movies and books that glorify conflict, and personal or professional engagements that tend to foster conflict or debate. It also includes self-driven conflict such as a need to be right, have the last word, be the best, and feel entitled.

- **No fear of death**. While the fear of death is commonly vanquished especially for near-death experiencers who know the exquisite love and relief that abounds across the veil, it is also commonly eliminated or lessened for the same reasons in those who have transformative events that don't involve any sense of death.

- **Trust in Divine inspiration and timing**. As we get more comfortable surrendering our need to demand specific outcomes or direction in our life, we begin to see evidence that trusting higher guidance leads to constantly surprising opportunities and realizations. The perfection of Divine timing and manifestation becomes irrefutable. New doors open, healing perspectives abound, and fear plummets.

- **Increased comfort with new abilities**. For those who realized new abilities through their STE, it can take a while to feel at ease and confident in working with these new skills. With time we reach a stage where it feels natural to be more aligned with these abilities than with our fear and doubt, and sharing or utilizing them becomes a joyful endeavor.

Increased creativity. Being led more by our joy and Divine alignment, we often find ourselves drawn to more creative endeavors. This is in some ways how we use our voice to share our evolving perspectives or to convey the higher energies flowing within us.

- **Ability to make choices from a sense of freedom and joy rather than fear or obligation**. As we become more aware of our motivations for what we do or how we are living our life, we may realize we have been making choices out of a sense of safety or responsibility that do not align with our highest joy or newly liberated spirit. We begin to evaluate our home, work and community life and become more comfortable making choices that allow us to live more honestly.

- **Increasing resonance with others who are awakening**. As we become more comfortable living authentically aligned with our purpose and joy, we have less interest in being around others who do not foster contentment or inspire our Divine potential. We find ourselves drawn to those who understand and celebrate our greater perspectives.

- **Less worry about what others think of us**. Related to the above, as we settle into a more authentic life we have less need for validation of our STE or our self from outside sources. We are less invested in external gratification such as flattery, accolades, or praise, and feel no need to measure ourselves against others.

- **Peace with decision to stay or leave relationship, job, community**. The more we become centered in a deeply honest state of being, the more we feel comfortable ensuring that the primary influences in our life foster alignment with our truth. For many this means leaving situations that do not feel supportive, resonant, or joyful, and for others it means finding ways to remain in the situation on different terms.

PART TWO

AWAKENING WITHOUT SPIRITUALLY TRANSFORMATIVE EXPERIENCES

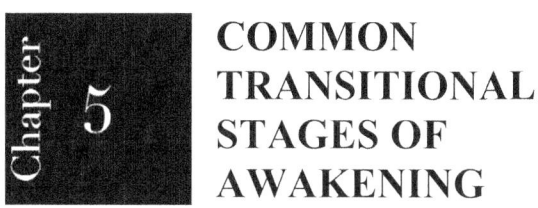

COMMON TRANSITIONAL STAGES OF AWAKENING

Transitional stages of awakening that occur without spiritually transformative experiences come with their own unique challenges. We usually have nothing to point to as a cause for feeling *different*; we just know that something in us has shifted.

Awakenings that occur gradually rather than through the jolt of an STE commonly reach pivotal stages, including:

> **Realization that something needs to change.** We feel that where we are or what we are doing in our life is no longer aligning with who we are now. This awareness feels different than simply maturing out of a phase, drifting apart in a marriage, or broadening our professional interests or goals. It feels more like we are literally waking up to the deep realization that we simply cannot live our life the same way we used to. This stage often comes with heightened chaos or frustrations that compound the feeling that something needs to change.

> **Feeling stuck.** While we know something needs to change — usually a relationship, job, or community that no longer feels tolerable — we cannot sense what that change actually needs to be or how to bring it about. It is one thing to want out of a situation, it is a whole other thing to know where to go next. Without a clear sense of

direction we can feel trapped, lost, or paralyzed. We often realize in this phase that fear is playing a big role in our inability to see a way forward: fear of making the wrong decision, or of financial insecurity, or of the unknown, and so on.

➢ **Significant change is happening out of our control**. This is sometimes referred to as "dark night of the soul." This can be a deeply confusing and painful time in which change happens unpredictably and dramatically. We can feel thrown off balance repeatedly and cannot seem to find stability in ways that were once reliably available. For some this stage passes within months, for others it can go on for years.

> *"Many times the dream state is when a stronger pull towards awakening starts showing up."*

➢ **A sense of self that no longer feels tolerable**. This is a common challenge for people who have long held at bay a truth about themselves, but it is also common for people who have lived for many years strongly identified with fear, discontent, victimhood, or responsibility for others over themselves. We have an inking in this stage that we are being powerfully called to live *freely*, and that call is making us honestly face whatever obstructions block our path to that freedom.

➢ **Frustration or exhaustion with having been on a spiritual path for years with seemingly no progress or transformative events**. This is an especially common challenge for people who have studied different philosophies and/or followed multiple spiritual teachers for many years and never had any real "aha!" that brought about a visceral or lasting sense of Divine connection. Understandings have remained more intellectual or theoretical, when what we deeply yearn for is *experiential* knowing. There can be doubt about whether spiritual teachings are even true if there has never been experiential evidence, and we may begin to ask ourselves, "What's the point of all this?"

➢ **Deep yearning to connect with Divine Love or Higher Power**. For many people, regardless of how long their spiritual journey has been, the yearning to connect to the Divine becomes almost incessant. It feels like we cannot get the desire for connection out of our system, and yet that connection remains elusive.

➢ **Lingering depression, grief, and/or anxiety**. These are often the very signs that make us pay attention to the lack of spiritual fulfillment in our life situation, but they can also manifest or increase as a result of that lack of fulfillment. These feelings commonly escalate the longer we live in limbo without a clear path forward and an unsated desire for Divine connection.

➢ **Dreams that feel like callings**. Many times the dream state is when a stronger pull towards awakening starts showing up. Some people begin to encounter angels or messages or otherworldly realms that feel like an invitation into, or a sign of, higher awareness. The feelings incited in these dreams are usually unshakable, as though they are demanding that we pay attention. (Note there are peri-sleep states where spiritually transformative events can occur, and these are different than dream states. In dream events you are generally not aware you are dreaming. In hypnagogic events you are aware you are not dreaming but also not in a normal awake state.)

Chapter 6
TIPS TO MANAGE TRANSITIONAL STAGES OF AWAKENING

Awakening without a catalyzing transformative event can be a powerful lesson in surrender and trust. Either by choice or by circumstances we eventually realize the path to relieving our unsettledness is also the path to our higher potential. That path is illuminated by authentic surrender of our chronic fruitless efforts to figure out how to control our direction, and a willingness to trust that higher guidance will lead us to higher potential. Contrary to what our mind believes about this, we are not surrendering our power or our free will. We are surrendering TO our true power and allowing our free will to align with Divine will. At some point we accept that we either have to take a leap of faith and make a change, or we have to put aside our demands for a specific future and lean into the present moment in full allowance. Either way, we *become available* to something more aligned with our highest interest and life purpose. And our mind cannot know or predict what that is.

> *"The construction of our unique energetic field is like scaffolding that has been arranged in a design that holds us in a particular way"*

Key to managing transitional stages of awakening is understanding that we have for far too long demanded that our precious mind tell us who we are and how to stay safe in that limited self-identity. All of our questions, doubts, confusion, fears, frustrations, strategies, disappointments, story angles and analyses are crafted by, and held in, our mind. And what we are being called into in our awakening is all that is available to us beyond all the old thoughts through which our mind operates. Our addiction to identifying with our thoughts, and our entrenched habit of believing those thoughts, keeps our focus firmly in the mental sphere. But the pull that is taking us into awakening is the yearning for the direct experience with the Divine, and for that we have to *be available* to greater awareness.

To use a simple analogy, imagine a drop of water in the ocean that believes it is something other than water and separate from its source, the ocean. It believes it is a singular entity all alone in a vast environment, and it desperately yearns to be in union with water. It bobs around in its little sense of self obsessively thinking about how to keep itself safe in its big ocean, how to succeed there, how to be good enough there, all while constantly deeply yearning to be connected to water. It lives its life *focused through the lens* of a single thought that its mind believes is true: I am separate from water. Its entire identity and existence is oriented in thoughts based in *separation* consciousness. All the while the drop is water, immersed in and inseparable from its source. But as long as the drop remains oriented in, and focused through, the mind that believes it is not water, it is unavailable to the direct experience of *being* water. It cannot remain doggedly focused in separation and be available to the experience of union. And this is what we keep trying to do as humans who yearn to be in union with Source.

Using our separation-oriented mind to try to sort through and strategize our way into an aligned life in which Divine understanding and connection flow naturally is like pushing on a door that says pull. *Efforting* through thought is an opposing force on the allowance of realization. While we obsessively analyze, expect, anticipate and question, we are leaning against the very door we are trying to open. (This is in part why we can more easily have epiphanies in the shower; as we tune into the feel of warm water we naturally relax our efforts to think and are in a greater state of allowance.)

Understanding all of this, we can see why many of the ways to most easily navigate transitional stages of awakening help us reorient our *way and state of being*. Helpful ways to shift into a more steady state of allowance and trust include:

◎ **Allow quiet time in different environments on a regular basis**. Getting out of our daily work and home environments and routines can be very helpful. Nature is especially good for this because it is a space of no resistance or expectation, so we have plenty of room to just *be*. It also helps to do self-retreats, like a week alone in a cabin or at the beach. This is not meant to be quiet time to sort through our problems, but time alone to *be available* to our own inner wisdom and guidance.

◎ **Explore various meditation techniques.** Meditation is the most common way to calm the mind, but very few people find it easy to do. This is in part because we usually approach it with trepidation, but also because we may not be practicing a technique that is most natural for us. Some techniques help us calm or quiet the mind, others help us redirect or interrupt impulsive patterns of the mind, and others help us go beyond the mind to access expanded awareness. It helps if we approach meditation from a place of curiosity and exploration, and try different methods to see what feels most comfortable or helpful. Common meditation techniques include:

> - Follow the breath
> - Transcendental
> - Chanting sounds and mantras
> - Guided or visualization
> - Mindfulness
> - Chakra
> - Loving kindness
> - Relaxation
> - Silent
> - Movement (e.g. whirling from the Sufi tradition)

◎ **Base little decisions on your contentment**. This can be an extremely effective way to break the habit of making decisions from a place of lack, responsibility, or fear. Asking ourselves "does this delight me?" or "does this feel nurturing?" when deciding small things — what to have for lunch, what keychain to buy, where to put the sofa — can condition us to be mindful of what drives our decision making. We can fairly quickly see that, in making bigger life decisions we have not been prioritizing our contentment. Through this simple inquiry process we begin to choose with mindful intention, and this reorients our mind into following what most naturally aligns with our spirit. Eventually this way of being becomes our default, and the more consistently aligned we are, the easier Divine connection and a Divinely guided life becomes. So, even though it may sound cliché, the simple guidance here is:

FOLLOW YOUR DAMN JOY.

◎ **Create new movement in your energetic field**. Our body, mind and spirit operate in an energetic field; a rich infrastructure of vibrational patterns that give us our unique experience of life and identity. The construction of our unique field is like scaffolding that has been arranged in a design that holds us in a particular way as we go through life. The patterns of that scaffolding are created by many things, including our conditioned ways of thinking, reactionary impulses, and beliefs — all of which are being called into question in our spiritual awakening. Our field is shifting in varying degrees all the time, but old entrenched patterns tend to be less malleable and this makes fundamental changes to our old ways of being more difficult. Therefore it can be extremely helpful to create more openness and movement in our energetic field, helping us to release old patterns and allow new, more expanded energies to flow within us. This shift happens naturally through suggestions mentioned previously, but there are other ways to incite energetic openness, including:

- **Travel to new places.** Stepping into new environments is a great way to shake up stagnant energetic patterns. As we immerse ourselves in new places and engage with new people or cultures we allow the influence of different perspectives and thoughts. This gives our overworked mind a break from old habitual thoughts and allows our consciousness to expand effortlessly.

- **Explore creative endeavors.** Creative endeavors such as painting, writing, sculpting, coloring, crafting and so on help relax our focus out of the mind and into the allowance of *flow*.

- **Listen to different music.** Music is all about vibrational patterns, so introducing new vocal or instrumental influences into our awareness naturally moves our energetic field by infusing new vibrational patterns throughout.

- **Explore movement practices.** Movement practices such as qi gong, tai chi, and yoga help relax both our mind and our energetic field while also calmly moving energies within us. This can be especially helpful for people who struggle with being high-strung or chronically anxious. Alternatively, dance is a great way to relax the mind and move energies within us in a more expressively cathartic way.

- **Explore energy and vibration-based support modalities.** There are many helpful energy and vibration-based modalities emerging now that can have a powerful effect on our mind, body and spirit. Energy work such as acupuncture, craniosacral therapy, reiki and EFT tapping can unstick old energetic patterns and create greater flow. Sound baths, vocal toning, biofield tuning, and gong ceremonies can drench our energetic field in powerful vibrations, creating significant openings and shifts. (I personally had a spontaneous healing of lifelong deafness in one ear during a gong ceremony.)

> *"Exposure to guides and communities that are oriented in direct experience can incite powerful energetic openings."*

◎ **Explore spiritual teachings that focus less on information and more on innate present-moment wisdom.** This is an exceptionally helpful way to relieve our over-burdened mind, which obsessively seeks to analyze, question and try to hold on to information that is primarily rooted in the past. Experiential present-moment teachings and guidance bring us out of a mental focus on past or future and into the energy field within us where innate wisdom and connection *is*. To be clear, this suggestion is not to say that information-centric teachings are wrong or not helpful; many are beautiful and profound. It is only to say that including more present moment-based teachings in our repertoire can greatly support the myriad internal shifts at play in transitional stages of awakening.

◎ **Explore mystic wisdom guides and communities that empower and incite direct experience**. Related to the previous point, exposure to guides and communities that are oriented in direct experience can incite powerful energetic openings because they work in higher vibrational fields rather than the dense cluttered field of the mind. Mystically-guided teachings are usually channeled or based in metaphysical experience; they are grounded in present-moment awareness and often delivered in group settings that amplify both the experience and the impact. These communities focus much more on the *experience and application* of Divine wisdom than intellectual analysis of the wisdom. It is important, however, that explorations with these types of guides and communities be approached with an intention to enhance our innate capacities and cultivate our innate wisdom, not with an expectation that they must deliver big metaphysical experiences. As has been mentioned previously, expectation is an exerting force that can block access to what is readily available in a state of allowance; again, like pushing on a door that says pull.

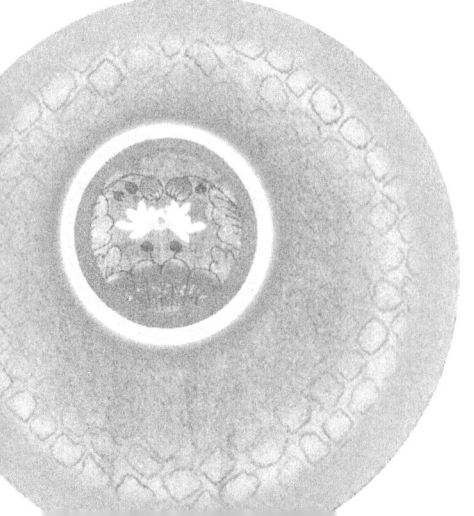

CAUTION WORTH REPEATING ABOUT MYSTIC WISDOM GUIDES AND COMMUNITIES: Today there are many people claiming to be mystics and channels who offer teachings and host communities, and some are very skilled and insightful in their service. However, mystics, channels, and the communities they host are prone to the same struggles with awakening that you are. While their intentions may be to serve, often times what is doing the serving is more ego than truth gleaned from Source. This can create complications for anyone who puts their trust in these individuals, especially when one is already confused in their awakening journey. Authentic mystic wisdom guides do not lead through fear, exploitation, manipulation, or guess work. They do not put themselves on a pedestal to be revered, and they do not mandate that you turn your decision making or life path over to them. Authentic mystic wisdom guides aim to empower others. They foster remembrance of, and resonance with, the Divine wisdom we all innately hold within. And they guide their communities in this same empowering way. So, trust what resonates and pay attention to any warning signs that may indicate disempowerment, exploitation, manipulation, or ineptitude. Let YOUR truth, YOUR power be your guide.

◎ **Consider allopathic medications for support if your body and mind become exhausted**. Many people eschew antidepressants and other allopathic treatments, but in some cases they can be a helpful temporary resource to get us through extreme periods of depression or confusion.

In addition to the tips already listed, there are countless resources that can provide more personalized support or specific information for you. To mention just a few:

- Books that are channeled or are inspired by direct embodied experiences can comfort, ground, and inspire us along our awakening journey — not just with information but with highly charged energetic resonance. Paul Selig's series of books are excellent for this, as are my own. (For both of us, start with our first books). The potent poetry of Chelan Harkin's *Susceptible to Light* is also wildly inspiring. For those who relate to more religious-based language, many people find Sebastián Blaksely and Mari Perron books helpful. (Note that there are countless books available that address awakening through unique voices or from unique perspectives such as angelic realms or animal guides or galactic counsels. I have never read these and I do not work in these ways, but that does not mean these books are not helpful. If you feel compelled to explore these, go for it.)

- Online programs such as Next Level Soul and Buddha at the Gas Pump (BATGAP) explore the subject of spiritual awakening from a wide variety of angles. The stories and discussions in these types of programs can help you see your own journey in a different light, and they can help you identify mystic wisdom guides that feel resonant. Their guests can also lead you to helpful resources such as techniques, courses and healing modalities. The discussion on BATGAP can at times be more intellectual but there are guests who speak quite inspiringly about their personal experiences, and the BATGAP website includes a categorical index of interviewees that includes psychotherapists and wisdom teachers/guides who are well versed in spiritual awakening.

- The Washington Center for Consciousness Studies (meditatelive.com) can be great for those who feel drawn to explore meditation through the lens of the more metaphysical eastern traditions. Dr. Rudy Bauer offers many free meditation videos and opportunities to meditate virtually with others on a daily basis.

- Suicide hotlines and crisis support are available if your despair gets to be too much. Wikipedia provides worldwide contact information for suicide hotlines at en.wikipedia.org/wiki/List_of_suicide_crisis_lines. Renowned sound healer Tom Kenyon has a suicide prevention program that works to ease the brain patterns contributing to despairing thoughts (tomkenyon.com/suicide-prevention). For those dealing with particularly relentless depression, medications may be a helpful bridge to get you through peak intense times, and these should be discussed with your mental health provider.

WHAT TO LOOK FORWARD TO

As the transitional stages of awakening begin to ease into a steadier state of comfort and acceptance, you will discover many of the same shifts that those who experience transformative events do, including:

- **Comfort in trusting Divine inspiration and timing.** As we get more comfortable surrendering our need to demand specific outcomes or direction in our life, we begin to see evidence that trusting higher guidance leads to constantly surprising opportunities and realizations. The perfection of Divine timing and manifestation becomes irrefutable. New doors open, healing perspectives abound, and fear recedes.

- **Ability to make choices from a sense of freedom and joy rather than obligation or fear.** As we grow accustomed to living more authentically aligned with our Divine nature and making decisions based in contentment, freedom and joy become our default motivations for what we choose to do and how we choose to live.

- **Peace with decision to stay or leave relationship, job, community.** Related to the above, the more we become centered in a deeply honest state of being, the more comfortable we feel in ensuring that the primary influences in our life foster alignment with our truth. For many this means leaving situations that do not feel supportive, resonant, or joyful, and for others it means finding ways to remain in the situation on different terms.

Deeper ability to accept self, others, and situations. Our old impulses of judgment usually become much less intense or frequent. We have a greater capacity to accept people and circumstances as they are rather than needing them to be different to make us feel better. This process begins with heightened awareness that our old reactionary habits have waned, and we grow evermore aware that we are evolving into a more gentle way of relating to self and others.

- **Ability to find more beauty and wonder in the world**. As our thoughts become less cluttered and judgmental, we greatly increase our ability to see more deeply into what is right before our eyes. We recognize and appreciate the weave of interdependence in our world, and how incredible it is to be part of, and blessed by, the interplay of all things.

- **Increased capacity to feel connected to Higher Self, Divine guides, and deeper wisdom**. As we become less focused through the mind from which our confusion has been generated and perpetuated, we find ourselves consistently dropping deeper into intuitive awareness. This is especially enhanced for those who feel drawn to meditative practices that quiet the mind and bring us into a more discerning state of internal awareness.

Remembrance of our playful nature. As our focus on frustration and thoughts continue to decrease we find ourselves naturally feeling more lighthearted and drawn to lighthearted influences. The more we relax our mind, the more we remember that we are, inherently, joyful beings. We feel more playful and see more whimsy in life.

PART THREE

GUIDANCE FOR PRACTITIONERS, SPIRITUAL LEADERS, AND MEDIA

GUIDANCE FOR PRACTITIONERS AND SPIRITUAL LEADERS

Chapter 8

I must begin this chapter with a reminder that the information I provide in this text comes solely from two decades of personal experience with spiritually transformative experiences and my work with people around the world in varying stages of spiritual awakening. I have been the one needing support from others and the one providing it to them. I have been outright rejected by religious institutions and spiritual centers because I am a mystic, and eagerly welcomed as their guest for the same reason. I have held in confidence countless stories from people wounded by individuals and communities they turned to for guidance in their awakening journey, and I have held in confidence countless stories from individuals and communities struggling to know how to authentically serve in these awakening times. I celebrate every important lesson learned and the greater potential being realized by all of us through these experiences. We are all stumbling our way through this powerful time of transformation together. Remembering this can help us travel this awakening path with more compassion and grace.

Before I delineate guidance for individual practitioners separately from spiritual leaders, I want to address one important bit of guidance that applies to both groups. It is important to realize that we are all being called to recover the key missing spirit in spirituality: BIG JOLLY LOVE.

Spiritual teachings, practices, environments, and support have historically been extremely somber.

Theology is heavily weighted in stories of death, conflict, hardship, morality and overcoming. Meditation teachers, yoga instructors, and body workers speak in subdued tones and say *namaste* in a way that implies Divine greetings are supposed to be solemn. Ministers and counselors encourage us to sort through our sins and sorrows, pray for forgiveness, and revere the great serious teachers and saints. Being spiritually oriented in this way has not cultivated or honored the playful loving nature of Source/God or ourselves. In fact, spirituality has kept our focus *away* from lighthearted sacred relationship. As a result:

***living with a repressed jolly spirit in a
deeply serious world has been exhausting.***

This is not to dismiss the hardships or sorrows we face in our human experience. On the contrary, the very idea of putting "jolly" in a spiritual context can help us understand how we contribute to our hardships and sorrows without realizing it. We have been conditioned to live oriented in a way that actively pushes our innocently playful Self away. This starts at a young age; we get all kinds of messages in our very serious world that tell us it is not safe to be vulnerable, so we begin shutting down our innocent, playful nature. Then, without realizing it, we gradually begin to grieve the loss of that part of ourselves, and that grief just adds to the heaviness we carry in our heart.

Spiritual awakening compels us to rediscover and reclaim more of our innate truth, and acclimate to living in that expanded awareness. BIG JOLLY LOVE is not only an innate Divine truth, it is a powerful doorway into to ever deeper truths. Therefore, the people and places we turn to for support and guidance can help us greatly by actively inciting, and being a presence of, this aspect of Source and their own Divine nature. This goes beyond just delivering services or sermons in an upbeat tone or sprinkling lighthearted platitudes on top of serious teachings. There is a reason the word BIG is included in the term BIG JOLLY LOVE. This aspect of Divine Love seeks to permeate the very essence of both practitioner and practice, messenger and message. It seeks to be the energy through which everything is engaging.

The task of liberated people is not to scold the world and preach to it, but to delight it back to its senses. ~**Alan Watts**

I cannot overstate what a powerful influence the radiance of BIG JOLLY LOVE is within ourselves and the world. This has been shown to me and to countless others I work with time and time again.

A few simple examples of how I have personally seen BIG JOLLY LOVE easily shift spiritual engagements and teachings include:

▷ I knew an elderly Catholic woman who grew tired of attending somber church-based funerals in which the vibe was more sadness than celebration. She also did not think it was fair that the dead person missed out on hearing what people said about them. So, she hired a Dixieland band and invited her friends, family, and priest to her wake while very much alive. She got to hear all the stories people would normally tell about her after she died, and she got to talk about all the things she loved about her life. She died a few years later having ensured that her death was not a somber event.

▷ While on a jam-packed speaking tour in south Texas, I was belatedly invited to give a talk at a spiritual center near several other locations at which I had engagements. The requested date was the only evening I had free, and I declined the offer because I knew I would not have the energy by that time to give another talk. But it happened that the date of the request was my birthday, so the inviting minister offered to host a party for me rather than ask me to speak. That was a much more fun idea and required no energy for me to be "on," so I accepted. The party turned into a spirited interactive evening of question and answer that was far more fun, personal, and impactful for the congregation than a talk would have been.

▷ Again and again I have witnessed for myself and others that greetings in Divine realms are absolutely NOT always solemn. It is usually something more akin to high-fiving your neighbor on the barstool next to you. Angels and masters are not wandering around Divine realms bowing and whispering "*Namaste*" to each other. A Divine greeting is a celebratory moment. It is Love seeing Love, which is a joyous occasion: "Oh hey! I know YOU! I honor YOU, beautiful Divine being!" When we intend to meet or see others authentically in their light, a joy springs forth from us naturally, and the other person can feel that resonance in their soul.

▷ Most of my own work now happens in collaboration with a collective of Divine guides called Consensus, whose numbers are so large they fill a stadium. They often bring people I work with into the stadium with them because, without any effort, the very idea of a stadium can evoke feelings of high energy, togetherness, cheering and joy. They regularly illuminate serious understandings in lighthearted ways in this setting (they like to say they are wise cheerleaders), but they also use this spacious container to compassionately hold the pain of others while illuminating higher perspectives and healing. So, not only do they teach through BIG JOLLY LOVE, their environment itself is that energy. This is not to say they do not offer teachings in serious ways; they do that regularly. It is to say that BIG JOLLY LOVE is an intentionally obvious part of *what they are*, and often it is that aspect of them that most easily facilitates Divine understanding and healing.

"We can help ourselves and each other find joy not just in, but through spirituality."

Many people who work with me are able to relax their mind enough to come into direct relationship with their Higher Self or Divine entities, and it is very common for them to have healing wisdom rise up from within themselves in surprisingly simple, lighthearted ways. I am not guiding them with any subliminal lighthearted imagery or ideas in this process, it just happens naturally. The clients are frequently reminded *from within* about the importance of, and the healing power of, letting life and love feel more playful. And this Divine guidance ALWAYS comes through in ways they cannot anticipate. A few simple examples[1]:

- A woman who had an oppressive Christian upbringing grew to resent Jesus, and as an adult she

---

[1] Two minor details have been changed to respect client confidentiality.

immersed herself solely in eastern religious studies and practices. Much to her surprise, in the stadium with Consensus she encountered Jesus, who was exuding exquisite love . . . while dancing a jig. The encounter was instantly healing, and it opened the door to wisdom within the client that could then flow from new perspectives.

- When a highly pedigreed executive burdened with anger was finally able to relax his mind enough, a heavenly choir appeared. The glowing choir members in white robes opened their mouths to sing and the client was expecting a great angelic hymn to spring forth, but instead they began raucously singing All You Need is Love by the Beatles. Because this energy was playing out within the client, it was as if old hardened patterns burst open and he began to cry deeply in relief.

- A lovely, gentle-spirited man who was feeling stuck in a boring life entered into the stadium and found himself seated amidst a very loud and lively Divine rock-n-roll band. When the man asked why he was greeted by this rowdy group, they said, "Because you forgot that joy can be very loud within you." With incredible simplicity they reconnected him to a side of his nature that reinvigorated his fervor for life.

We all have Consensus energy within us. These guides remind me frequently that they are simply higher and higher aspects of whoever they are gathering with. Those of us who support, guide, and facilitate spiritual awakening have an opportunity now to tap into the BIG JOLLY LOVE within us and be the presence of exuberant permission for all of us to be ALL that we really are, including our innocently playful Self.

We can help ourselves and each other find joy not just in, but *through* spirituality. We can be the force of BIG JOLLY LOVE that reorients ourselves, others, and communities out of heavy-heartedness and into relief and celebration. This is the new orientation that allows us far greater ease of being in the world, and allows the world itself to be more at ease.

TIPS FOR PRACTITIONERS SERVING AWAKENING INDIVIDUALS

In the early years of my awakening I saw more than forty therapists, doctors, energy workers, and healers of varying types all around the world as I was trying to get help with the myriad transformative events I kept having. While the majority of these practitioners had some measure of bias or judgment that clouded their ability to help me, the main challenge for all of them was a lack of understanding, training and resources necessary to work with someone like me. I still see this today in people who are confused or frustrated after seeking help from practitioners who were inexperienced in managing spiritual awakening challenges or who were biased or working from ego.

Fortunately, there are many new types of support modalities emerging now and a growing number of resources available to help practitioners who offer these services. These emerging resources can help us hone our skills, increase our understanding of the people we serve, and work from higher states of connection and guidance. This book is a resource specifically for the latter two points.

In addition to the wonderful variety of courses and books available to help expand understanding and hone skills in specific types of counseling, energy work, mediumship or other modalities, these tips can supplement that support and strengthen offerings:

➤ **Be aware of the range of things that awakening individuals are dealing with**. Through this book you can see there are many diverse factors at play for someone integrating a spiritually transformative experience or managing their way through transitional stages of awakening. Understanding the signs and range of challenges can help you ask insightful questions to glean where someone is in their journey — and to understand where they see themselves. This information can be extremely helpful in knowing how to work

> *"allow space for rapid evolution in clients and yourself"*

with the various factors at play in the person you are serving. This material can also help you realize the same signs and range of challenges you may be facing yourself.

➤ **People are waking up in leaps and bounds, and their needs can change just as much**. If you see clients on a regular basis, allow space for them to be in a state different than you expect each time. The same goes for yourself; you may in fact be able to offer your service more deeply or powerfully than you expect, so allow space for rapid evolution in clients and yourself.

➤ **Honor your unique innate gifts**. Some people aim for a laundry list of certifications in various techniques or modalities. There is nothing wrong with this, but remember that you have more to offer than just someone else's script or someone else's methods. Certified trainings can help you expand your knowledge or skills, but our awakening world is calling for you to bring your whole beautiful self to what you do. We need your personal touch; we need the unique way that BIG JOLLY LOVE flows through you; we need your unique skills of discernment and interpersonal attunement. Tap into the Divine You that is providing the service, not just the you whose trainings have been validated by others.

➢ **Set clear boundaries of what you can offer and what is not in your intended scope of service**. Awakening individuals will come to you for a multitude of reasons, many of which they may not even be able to articulate. By being clear about what you do or do not offer, you help clients know what they can come to you for and what your boundaries are in case they come with other expectations. For example, I state outright on the Consultations page of my website that I do not connect people with their love ones who have passed, because this is something many

"We are called to be more compassionate with ourselves now, not just with others."

people are looking for. This connection does, in fact, happen in rare occasions in my consultations but it is always a surprise and not by my intention. If I don't address this common expectation upfront, I risk inciting hope in someone who is very likely grieving, and I am very likely to deepen their grief if the connection to their loved one does not happen.

➢ **Design both the schedule and the volume of your offerings around what genuinely nourishes your spirit**. Without realizing it, practitioners often develop their model of service guided more by fear than trust, more by responsibility than joy, and more by ego than Divine inspiration. We have been conditioned to believe that working 5 days a week, 8 hours a day is normal, when in fact what may provide more freedom, creative inspiration and potential for you is 3 days a week, 4 hours a day. We have been conditioned to believe that more work equals more abundance, when in fact abundance can come through greater availability to Divine supply in myriad forms. We have been conditioned to be shy about assigning value to our time or service, when in fact the value of our time and service is the very thing Divinely taking care of us. Maybe seeing fewer clients for longer periods of time feels better than stacking them one after another hour after hour. Maybe instead of offering one-time appointments you require clients to commit to a series of sessions because this aligns with your intention to ensure sustaining impact. Maybe you work more intuitively connected in the afternoons, or you feel more joyful working from home, or you need entire months off to recharge. When you align your schedule with your own highest joy, nurturance, rhythms, and ease, you ensure you are in highest service to self and our awakening world.

➤ **Find your true Divine center and let that be your guide relentlessly.** Many awakening people are changing careers and becoming service providers. If you are just starting out, be mindful to allow yourself plenty of time to get grounded in, and guided by, higher truth and opportunities. Often people just starting out are driven more by a fear of lack or by an egoic desire to change others, and this can lead to offering services before there is enough skill, or offering services that are simply not helpful. Take plenty of time to ground yourself in loving intention, and practice extensively with friends and family before going public. Importantly, approach every practice session with the same focus and boundaries you would have in a professional setting. In-person or online practice sessions over wine in your pajamas will not prepare you for someone in crisis who needs skilled care.

➤ **While we always want to meet clients where they are, we also need to remember that we are meeting them where we are as well.** If you are in a funk and things are just not grooving for you at the time of a client's appointment, it is okay to reschedule. The funky feeling may be an important signal that the timing is not right for you or for the client. Be honest with yourself and the client, and trust that better timing will be available when it is in the highest interest of all involved. This is much more helpful than the old way of doing business that was driven by obligation, forcing us to just trudge forward and try to make something happen. It is frustrating to all parties when a client shows up for a session they paid for and have been looking forward to, and the practitioner just can't be fully present. We are called to be more compassionate with ourselves now, not just with others.

➤ **If you are an intuitive service provider (channel, medium, Akashic reader, energy worker, etc.), remember that these services are still evolving and it is up to you to offer services responsibly.** There are no set standards for regulation, training or licensing for most intuitive modalities of support, therefore vulnerable clients can be harmed by unskilled or arrogant practitioners who overstep their bounds. If you are not trained in medical or mental health diagnosis, it can be both unethical and dangerous to outright diagnose a client with a condition or refute a diagnosis they have been given by trained medical and mental health

"Be clear about the limits of your knowledge."

professionals. Awakening individuals can have all manner of physical symptoms and be all over the place mentally as they are integrating their experiences or managing transitional stages. It can be very difficult to know all that is at play in someone's symptoms or behavior. Outright diagnosing a client can inflict more fear and confusion than they may already have, as well as trigger deeper issues with which you may be unaware. If you suspect a client has a particular condition, you can let them know of your *suspicions* if you feel that is necessary, but be clear about the limits of your knowledge. If you suspect a client may need licensed medical or mental health care, gently suggest they explore that avenue of support.

➤ **Talk to peers with more experience when necessary.** Related to the above, if you are a trained mental health professional and are starting to see more clients with signs of spiritual awakening (see chapters two and six), before you assume any particular diagnosis it can be helpful to talk with other professionals who are well versed in care for spiritually awakening clients. The Buddha at the Gas Pump website BATGAP.com and the Spiritual Emergence Network website www.spiritualemergence.org are both excellent referral resources. You can also check with your state or national associations for these peers as well. This same guidance holds true for all practitioners: if you are supporting a client through a complex or new-to-you issue, it can be extremely helpful to talk with peers who have more experience or expertise in your field of work than you do.

➢ **Many therapists and counselors are starting to realize that the traditional psychotherapeutic and talk-based models are too limiting to work with people who are struggling with spiritual awakening**. Approaches that only engage the mind can be problematic for clients for whom it would be more helpful to go inward for clarity and calm. Therapists and counselors themselves are often finding the same challenge from their side — they seek to focus less on talk and more on discovering what healing perspectives are available in quiet internal awareness. State and national mental health associations can address this evolving challenge by engaging in open dialogue with their members about the realities of our awakening world, and prioritizing research on new psycho-spiritual methodologies. (This is slowly starting to happen.) And practitioners can be a great help to these associations and to each other by speaking up about their experiences in working with clients in spiritual crisis or confusion, and/or about the professional challenges they are having as a result of their own spiritual awakening.

> For therapists who are working with people with awakening experiences and want to start the process of educating themselves more, helpful books to read include *Spiritual Emergency* by Stan Grof and *Breaking Open: Finding a Way Through Spiritual Emergencies* by Jules Evans and Tim Read.

INFORMATION FOR SPIRITUAL LEADERS

Spiritual communities are in the eye of the awakening storm and everywhere along its path. Community models are changing rapidly, with more individuals leading private groups and more organizations grappling with how to best serve their awakening (and often dwindling) congregations. Individuals leading their own communities are playing the role of group facilitator while also vulnerably awakening through, and right in front of, their groups. And organizational leaders, their staff, and the umbrella associations to which they belong are all part and parcel of collective support and collective confusion as they, too, are all at different levels of awakening.

Traditional models of spiritual fellowship, support, and guidance are not withstanding the expansion of consciousness and Divine connection that spiritual awakening is compelling. Even in the countless progressive spiritual centers I visited in my speaking tours I heard from so many leaders who were deeply frustrated by the limitations they were forced to operate within because of outdated organizational boundaries and ideologies. And that energy of frustration and limitation radiated right out into the congregations, where the needs of the people were the exact opposite. It was blatantly obvious which leaders were able to — or doggedly determined to — do their work with joyful flexibility and which ones were not. And the corresponding sense of spacious joy, or absence thereof, was palpable in their congregations.

> *"The more you allow the Divine as you to be both messenger and message, the more impactful your service can be."*

Individuals who lead their own private communities often face this same challenge when they do not trust themselves enough to let their leadership and offerings evolve at the same pace they themselves are. They can have a fear of not being able to predict or navigate the unknown, or a concern that their community members may not be ready for information or capacities that are becoming more apparent in them. I went through this personally when my work shifted from offering teachings based on the wisdom I gleaned in my own metaphysical experiences to having to trust my ability to channel Consensus, the large collective of beings that started coming through me twenty years after my awakening journey began.

Following are tips that can help spiritual community leaders who are reshaping their leadership, organizations, and offerings to help meet the ever-shifting needs of our awakening world:

> **Let the voice that speaks in your leadership role be sourced from all aspects of your Divine nature, especially BIG JOLLY LOVE.** If you are not feeling truly buoyed by your teachings or sermons, or you are not uplifted by the very way in which you deliver those teachings or sermons, that dampened or repressed energy is imbued in the messages you are delivering. The more you allow the Divine as you to be both messenger and message, the more resonant and impactful your service can be. This requires that you check your spiritual ego and prioritize the exploration of, and trust in, your own Divine truths — and then put those truths front and center with your congregation, board of directors, donors and volunteers. For some leaders, this may, in fact, result in you having to leave the community you currently lead, but you will have planted an important seed of change in the fertile soil you leave behind and freed yourself up to serve more authentically.

> **Remember that you or your center may be the first place someone who is awakening turns to for support**. This means that all leaders and staff need to know how to hold safe space for awakening individuals. It is important that you let people know they will be met unconditionally where they are, even if you or your staff are not in the same place. Through this book you can see there are numerous things at play for someone integrating an STE and managing their way through transitional stages of awakening. Understanding the signs and range of challenges can help you listen with an open heart, ask insightful questions, and consider how to keep them grounded in love. This material can also help you realize the same signs and range of challenges you or your staff may be facing as well.

> **Be prepared to handle shifting community dynamics**. While awakening individuals face a range of challenges that require gentle understanding and support, so too can those who do not feel they are awakening fast enough. As community members come forward to share their transformative experiences or journeys, this can cause other members to feel jealous or judgmental, or make them believe they have somehow failed or are unworthy of such gifts. Remind your community members that the ego can cause all manner of confusion for everyone in these times. It will be important to speak openly and frequently about how everyone is on their own unique journey, and every stage is important not only to the individual but to the collective as a whole. If everyone woke up the same way our world would be a mess! One who awakens slowly or methodically may be unwittingly providing stability for themselves, their loved ones, and the collective, or they may be on a personal journey that is more about depth of key life themes than breadth of vast experiences.

> *"Awakening experiences may be driving some people out of traditional spiritual institutions, but it is also driving some people into them."*

> **Normalize awakening**. Related to the above, by speaking openly about awakening with your staff and congregants, and encouraging everyone to recognize the signs and challenges involved, you can shift the tone of the topic away from stigma, fear, and confusion and into an upbeat tone of celebration and

wonder. For leaders who have had STEs themselves, facing your own fear of judgment or ostracism and speaking your truth can be a powerful catalyst for needed change within your organization. Remember, the lineage of spiritual tradition(s) upon which your center was founded originated in mysticism. Mysticism — direct *experiential* knowing — is as old as spirituality, and we are called to bring this direct experiential knowing out of the realm of "ancient wisdom" and into the realm of "present knowing."

➢ **Let your awakening community members add to the Divine wisdom you share**. For every spiritual lesson you quote from a book or notable teacher, there is likely an equally powerful *embodied experience* of a spiritual lesson being held as a secret within some of your community members. As you normalize awakening and create safe space for people to share their awakening experiences, you will find that Divine wisdom is available and rising up evermore in present-moment awareness. Be curious about the wisdom gleaned in those who have had STEs; learn the details, the perspectives, the impact, and you will see these things beautifully illuminate and confirm spiritual teachings found in ancient texts. This is especially important in churches and other organized spiritual centers. Awakening experiences may be driving some people out of traditional spiritual institutions, but they are also driving some people into them — so use the blessing of these gifts. By inviting awakening congregants to contribute to the wisdom shared from the pulpit, you ensure the mobilization of ever-greater awakening potential throughout your communities.

> **Global and national spiritual associations can address changes needed in their organizational affiliates by prioritizing open dialogue about the support and resources their members need to robustly serve a rapidly awakening world**. Spiritual leaders can be a great help to these associations and to each other by speaking up about the challenges they face in working with communities that are yearning more for Divine *experience* and not just information. They can also help by speaking openly about their own yearning to lead from deeper personal Divine connection — to be more of an *embodied messenger*.

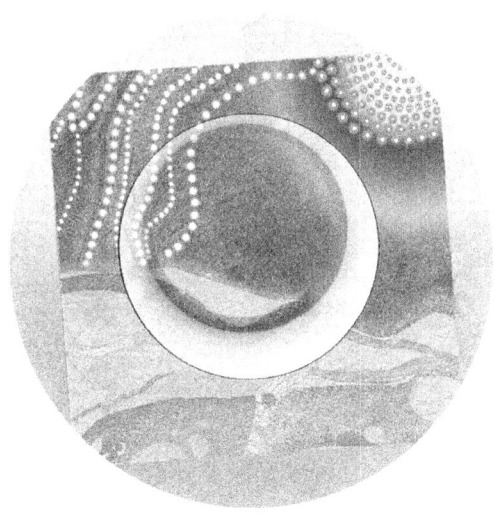

GUIDANCE FOR MEDIA REPRESENTATIVES

Chapter 9

For those who serve our awakening world through public media platforms: THANK YOU. You have the power to help mobilize our evolution in healing and inspiring ways on a global scale, so your work is incredibly important to our awakening journeys. I recognize and enthusiastically celebrate your contribution to humanity at this exciting time!

Every day more and more people are coming out with their incredible awakening stories, and every day more and more people are creating podcasts, publications, or other media outlets to explore these stories. Many well-established programs are expanding their focus to include discussions about awakening as well. I have been an interviewee on a variety of these programs, and occasionally I contribute articles to publications that focus on spiritual matters. I have also provided consultations for people who are spiritual program hosts and/or guests, and who are publishers of, or contributors to, spiritual materials. I offer these tips based on all of these experiences:

➤ **When interviewing an STE experiencer, understand that they can be extremely vulnerable and may still be integrating their experience or still learning how to talk about what happened**. As you can see in the first part of this book, individuals awakening through STEs are dealing with a wide variety of issues. Seek to understand not just the wisdom they gleaned in their experience but how it impacted their life and whether they have a sense of wellbeing now. This information will be helpful for your audience in many ways, especially since many of them have faced, or will soon be facing, some of the same issues as your guest.

➢ **Remember that an STE does not give us all the wisdom in the universe**. Experiencers are not able to honestly answer *from directly embodied experience* questions that require perspectives beyond the scope of their STE — but as a guest they may feel pressured to try. Ask questions that help you recognize the range of understandings your guests gleaned in their transformative event, and know that anything outside of that can be either uncomfortable for them or opening the door to ego-led discussion. The same holds true for questions aimed at philosophical or hypothetical debate. For example, asking "How do you think the Egyptian pyramids were built?" to someone whose STE simply gave them a blissful blast of God's love may be fun, but it is not bringing out the true gifts of their personal experience. If you host a show that fosters suppositional discussion, let the interviewee know that ahead of time and invite them to feel free to say when they do not feel comfortable with that line of discourse.

> *"An STE does not automatically make us experts on matters such as meditation or the rise of women behind the pulpit."*

➢ **An STE does not automatically give us the ability to write authoritatively about a broad range of spiritual subjects**. Related to the above, an STE does not automatically make us experts on matters such as meditation or the rise of women behind the pulpit —

but many experiencers may feel compelled to try because they feel honored to be asked. If you invite us to contribute articles, know what our areas of expertise are and the limited range of our experiences.

➢ **If you suspect a guest who is speaking about their STE is getting led off track by their ego, ask questions that help the interviewee see that**. This does not need to be done in a "gotcha" or accusing way, but in a compassionate way of "how do you feel we can we discern when…". This can help your audience see that this is a real challenge that experiencers have to deal with, and they can also identify when they may in fact do the same thing themselves.

➢ **Know that those of us who have had STEs can tell when we are being used to promote someone else's agenda**. The problem here is not just that it is exploitive, it is also that the gifts available through our experiences are being reduced or missed altogether because the host is trying to reshape or co-opt them for their own purpose. If you have a framework or lens through which you are going to interview a guest because it helps promote your book, course, events, or niche brand, be clear about that upfront so the guests can decide whether or not they want to be part of your promotional strategy.

The frameworks in which we share our stories and journeys are important. Spiritually transformative experiences and awakening journeys catalyze perspectives grounded in healing, collaboration, and love. If the frameworks within which we are asked to share our experiences are centered in conflict and comparison, we are not being met where we are. There is a difference between defensively asking someone who experienced God's profound love how they think that a loving God allows the pain of war, and asking the experiencer if, or how, they feel the wisdom revealed in their STE could potentially help heal the origins of war.

➤ **Make our time together a collaboration**. Most of us are not coming on your show or being profiled in your publication because we want to be famous. It is because something profound and powerful happened with us and our experiences can help and inspire others who are awakening. Most of us do not go through media training or have public relations teams to package us up nice and neat for the public. We are everyday people who are often just flying by the seat of our pants. Therefore, it is very helpful when hosts or their assistants tell us exactly what they need ahead of time and when they need it. Additionally, most of us are not experts in writing bios and taking head shots, so if you have tips that can help, or someone you can refer guests to who can help with such things, pass that information along. If you are particular about sound, lighting and camera position, also let us know ahead of time how to address these issues.

Remember that we are not simply guests who have an interesting story to share. Some of us are traumatized; some of us are still integrating our experiences and may still be a little disoriented; some of us are struggling with ego; some of us are scared of retribution, rejection, or expectations that we have to know more beyond what we gleaned from our experiences. But no matter what issues we may come with, we all have something to convey that can affect others deeply. We all carry energy that can help mobilize our awakening world. So we want to share our experiences carefully, respectfully, and truthfully. We want to share our stories well not just for ourselves or for you or even for the world. We want to share our stories well to honor Divine truth itself. We want to incite LOVE the way LOVE incited us. ♥

ACKNOWLEDGEMENTS

Heartfelt thanks to Patricia Pearce, Eleanor Kerlow, Corene Crossin, and Lisa Dewey for their early reviews of the manuscript and wise counsel. Thanks also to Dr. Amy Johnson, Lisa Wetsel, Isabell VanMerlin and Jacob King for their early read-throughs, feedback, and support.

The look and feel of this book is due to the big talents and even bigger heart of Cheri Warren. She made this book so much more than I could have imagined.

To get the full effect of the beautiful circle art provided by Rashani Réa visit her website at www.rashani.com.

Finally, this book was made possible by everyone who taught me about spiritual awakening from so many diverse angles over the years. From those who aimed to support me to those who allowed me to support them, this project has been a tribute to every lesson learned in our time together.

Printed in Great Britain
by Amazon

45813206R00056

Cultural Liturgies

VOLUME 3

Awaiting the King

Reforming Public Theology

James K. A. Smith

"Smith has written an essential guide to social life aimed at his fellow Christians but essential reading for all of his fellow citizens. His core insight, that the human being is created to pursue solidarity but must then be ceaselessly formed and re-formed to achieve and sustain it, is at least as bracing a critique of modern politics as it is of the deficiencies of political theology."
—YUVAL LEVIN, EDITOR OF *National Affairs* AND AUTHOR OF *The Fractured Republic*

"With characteristic verve and clarity—as well as honesty and nuance—this climactic volume of Smith's trilogy offers a broadly Augustinian perspective on public life that takes us beyond genealogy and modernity criticism. It is a much-needed intervention in evangelical political thought. Appreciative yet critical of contemporary alternatives, Smith offers a liturgical and missional focus that represents a distinctive contribution from a leading public theologian."
—ERIC GREGORY, PRINCETON UNIVERSITY

"Negotiating his way through the mass of confusions known as political theology, Smith has written a superb book that develops a constructive and nuanced position in the Reformed tradition. He has done so, moreover, by engaging in conversations with Oliver O'Donovan and Jeff Stout. This is a book that should be read widely by anyone interested in addressing the fundamental questions of church and politics."—STANLEY HAUERWAS, DUKE DIVINITY SCHOOL

"In this masterful work, Smith engages an impressive array of conversation partners as he explores the implications of the liturgical theology of culture he's developed throughout his Cultural Liturgies project for the public realm. The result is a constructive work of political theology that helps us imagine how to firmly root our political engagement in Christ while giving careful attention to the complex realities of our time."—KRISTEN DEEDE JOHNSON, WESTERN THEOLOGICAL SEMINARY; COAUTHOR OF *The Justice Calling*

"In *Awaiting the King*, Smith sets out to reform Reformed political theology. With his usual clarity, creativity, and verve, he accomplishes just that, hitting the right notes of both affirmation and critique by refocusing political theology on the *polis* of the church and its formative liturgical practices. *Awaiting the King* is a satisfying final movement in Smith's Cultural Liturgies symphony and a crucial contribution to the wider conversation in political theology."
—PETER LEITHART, PRESIDENT, THEOPOLIS INSTITUTE, BIRMINGHAM, ALABAMA

JAMES K. A. SMITH (PhD, Villanova University) is professor of philosophy at Calvin College, where he holds the Gary and Henrietta Byker Chair in Applied Reformed Theology and Worldview. He is also the editor of *Comment* magazine. A popular speaker, he has written many books, including *Desiring the Kingdom*, *Imagining the Kingdom*, and *You Are What You Love*.

Cover Art: *The Achievement of the Holy Grail by Sir Galahad, Sir Bors, and Sir Percival* (high-warp tapestry in wool and silk), Edward Coley Burne-Jones (1833–98)/Private Collection/Photo © Christie's Images/Bridgeman Images

Baker Academic
a division of Baker Publishing Group

Theology/Culture
ISBN 978-0-8010-3579-1

www.bakeracademic.com